Computer Training Series

Photoshop Essentials

Kevin Wilson

Luminescent Media

Photoshop Essentials

Kevin Wilson

Text and design © 2013 Luminescent Media

Find us on the web at www.luminescentmedia.co.uk
Contact us on office@luminescentmedia.co.uk

ISBN-13: 978-1484042571

ISBN-10: 1484042573

About The Author

Kevin Wilson, a practicing computer engineer and tutor, has been a computer buff for many years. After graduating with a masters in computer science, software engineering and multimedia systems, he has worked in the computer industry supporting and working with many different types of computer systems, worked in education running specialist lessons on film making and visual effects for young people.

He has also worked as an IT Tutor, has taught in colleges in South Africa and worked as a tutor for adult education in England.

Table of Contents

Photoshop

Before we get started, for purposes of this book, we will be working with a number of image files which can be downloaded from our website.

http://www.luminescentmedia.co.uk/freesamples.html

These resources are compressed into a zip file and you will need to extract them. Extract them to a folder in your pictures library.

Getting Started

Open Photoshop. Various tools and palettes are opened to help you manipulate images. We will briefly go over the Toolbox, the Tool Options Bar and the Palettes.

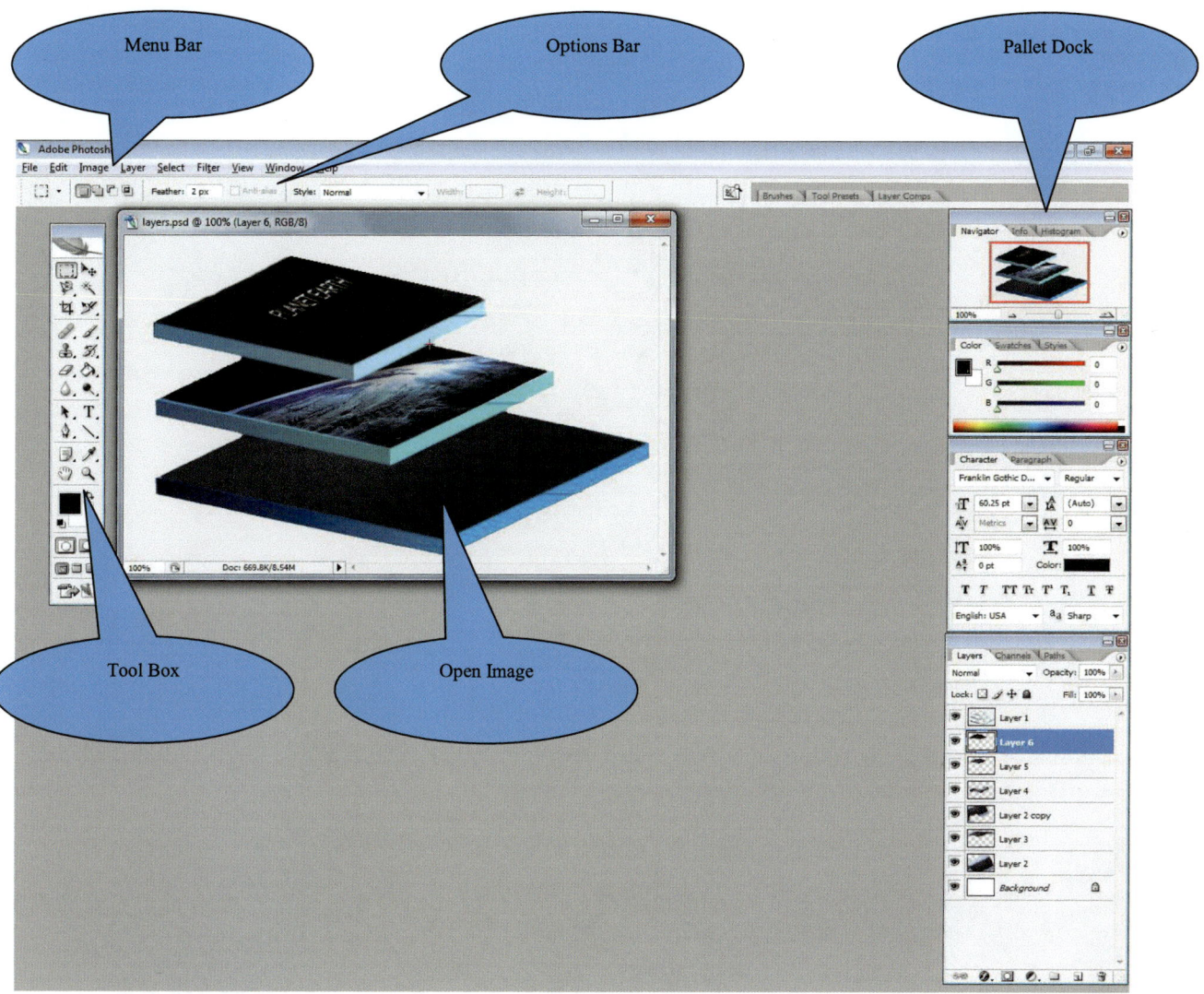

The Toolbox

In the Photoshop window, the toolbox appears on the left of the screen. As you can see, Photoshop has an enormous array of tools available to you. Many of these tools also have options that appear in the options bar at the top of the screen. The top six icons in the toolbox are known as the selection tools.

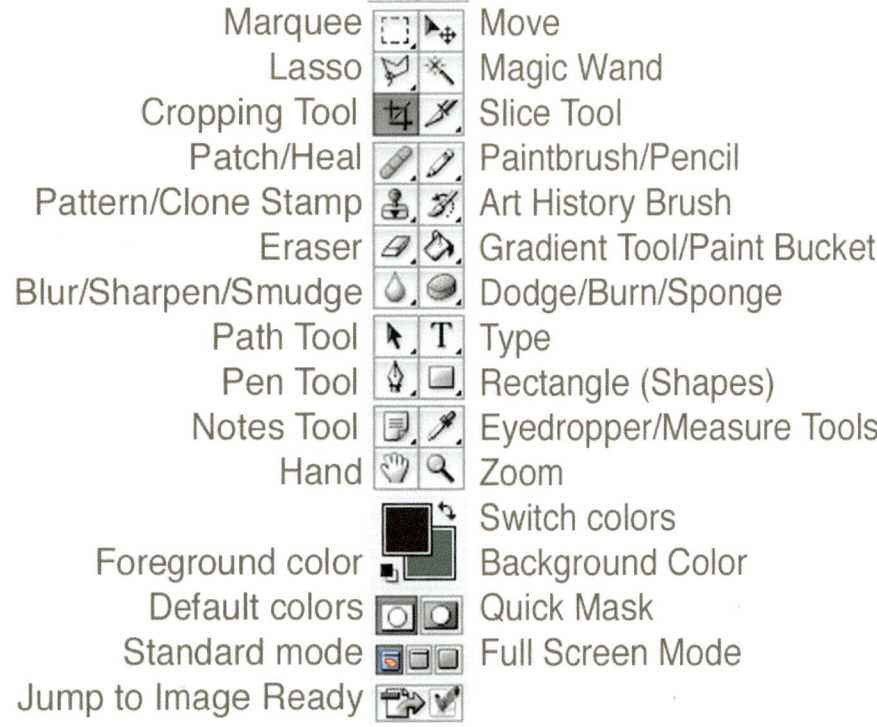

Additional related tools are indicated by a small arrow at the bottom right of the tool icon. These tools offer almost unlimited flexibility in working with an image.

Using these tools, and their submenus, you can select and move the entire image, a freehand portion of it, or all the pixels of a single colour. You can also make multiple selections by using the Shift key while dragging the mouse

Pen Tool

Photoshop includes a few versions of the pen tool. The pen tool creates precise paths that can be manipulated using anchor points. The freeform pen tool allows you to draw paths freehand, and with the magnetic pen tool, the drawn path attaches closely to outlines of objects in an image, which is useful for isolating them from a background.

Cropping

The crop tool can be used to select a particular area of an image and discard the portions outside of the chosen section. This tool assists in creating a focus point on an image and excluding unnecessary or excess space. Cropping allows enhancement of a photo's composition while decreasing the file size. By placing the cursor over the image, you can drag the cursor to the desired area. Once the Enter key is pressed, the area outside of the rectangle will be cropped. The area outside of the rectangle is the discarded data, which allows for the file size to be decreased.

Slicing

The slice tools, like the crop tool, are used in isolating parts of images. The slice tool can be used to divide an image into different sections, and these separate parts can be used as pieces of a web page. The slice select tool allows sliced sections of an image to be adjusted and shifted.

Moving

Once an area of an image is highlighted with the marquee tool, the move tool can be used to manually relocate the selected piece to anywhere on the canvas.

Marquee

The marquee tool can make selections that are single row, single column, rectangular and elliptical. An area that has been selected can be edited without affecting the rest of the image. Once the tool has been selected, dragging across the desired area will select it. The selected area will be outlined by dotted lines, referred to as "marching ants".

Lasso

The lasso tool is similar to the marquee tool; however, you can make a custom selection by drawing it freehand. There are three options for the lasso tool – regular, polygonal, and magnetic.

The regular lasso tool allows you to trace around your selection freehand. Photoshop will complete the selection once the mouse button is released. The user may also complete the selection by connecting the end point to the starting point. The "marching ants" will indicate if a selection has been made.

The polygonal lasso tool will only draw straight lines, which makes it an ideal choice for images with many straight lines. Unlike the regular lasso tool, you must continually click around the image to outline the shape. To complete the selection, you must connect the end point to the starting point just like the regular lasso tool.

Magnetic lasso tool is considered the smart tool. It can do the same as the other two, but it can also detect the edges of an image once the user selects a starting point. It detects the edge of an object by examining difference in pixels as the cursor move over the desired area. Closing the selection is the same as the other two, which should also should display the "marching ants" once the selection has been closed.

Quick Selection

The quick selection tool selects areas based on edges, similarly to the magnetic lasso tool. The difference between this tool and the lasso tool is that there is no starting and ending point. Since there isn't a starting and ending point, the selected area can be added on to as much as possible without starting over. By dragging the cursor over the desired area, the quick selection tool detects the edges of the image. The "marching ants" tell you what is currently being selected. Once done, the selected area can be edited without affecting the rest of the image.

Magic Wand

The magic wand tool selects areas based on pixels of a similar colour and intensity. You only need to click once, and this tool will detect pixels that are very similar to each other. When the image requires more than a few clicks, this tool doesn't work particularly well.

Eraser

The eraser tool will convert the pixels to transparent, unless it is the background layer. The size and style of the eraser can be selected in the options bar. This tool is unique in that it can take the form of the paintbrush and pencil tools. In addition to the straight eraser tool, there are two more available options – background eraser and magic eraser. The background eraser deletes any part of the image that is on the edge of an object. This tool is often used to extract objects from the background. The magic eraser tool deletes based on similar coloured pixels. It is very similar to the magic wand tool. This tool is ideal for deleting areas with the same colour or tone that contrasts with the rest of the image.

Text Tool

The text tool creates an area on a new layer where text can be entered, and creates vector-based text, so symbols, letters and numbers in various fonts and colours can be re-sized while maintaining the same quality.

Retouching

There are several tools that are used for retouching, manipulating and adjusting photos, such as the clone stamp, eraser, burn, dodge, smudge and blur tools.

The clone stamp tool samples a selected portion of an image, and duplicates it over another area using a brush that can be adjusted in size, flow and opacity.

The smudge tool, smudges the image when dragged over as if it was water colour paint.

The blur tool softens portions of an image by blurring the area.

The eraser tool removes pixels from an image, and the magic eraser tool selects areas of solid colour and erases them.

The burn and dodge tools, which are derived from traditional methods of adjusting the exposure on printed photos, have opposite effects; the burn tool darkens selected areas, and the dodge tool lightens them.

Healing tools

With improvement retouching tools like the Clone Stamp tool and Healing Brush tool, imperfections of an image can easily be removed. These tools essentially function by locating a source point or multiple source points that can be scaled or rotated in order to cover an imperfection or unwanted detail in a specific area of an image.

The clone stamp tool allows its user to replace one part of an image with another. If part of an original image is damaged, the damaged area can be restored by cloning a similar area from another image or within the current image. This tool works great for removing unwanted blemishes, such as acne and wrinkles, in a photograph.

To sample an image, the user must hold down the Alt key (PC) or the Option key (Mac) then click on the area. Once the sample area has been cloned, the user can drag the clone key to the desired area. An interesting feature about this tool is that it doesn't just sample within the size of the clone stamp, but it samples everything around it. The user can use this tool like a paintbrush to cover the desired area. Also, the user can clone in multiple areas without having to re-sample.

Tool Options Bar

At the top of the screen is the Tool Options Bar for example the paint brush selected below. When you select a tool from the toolbox, the parameters for using each tool appear in this menu bar for easy modification. So from the options bar you can change paint brush size, shape, etc. Or for the text tool you can change the font and colour etc.

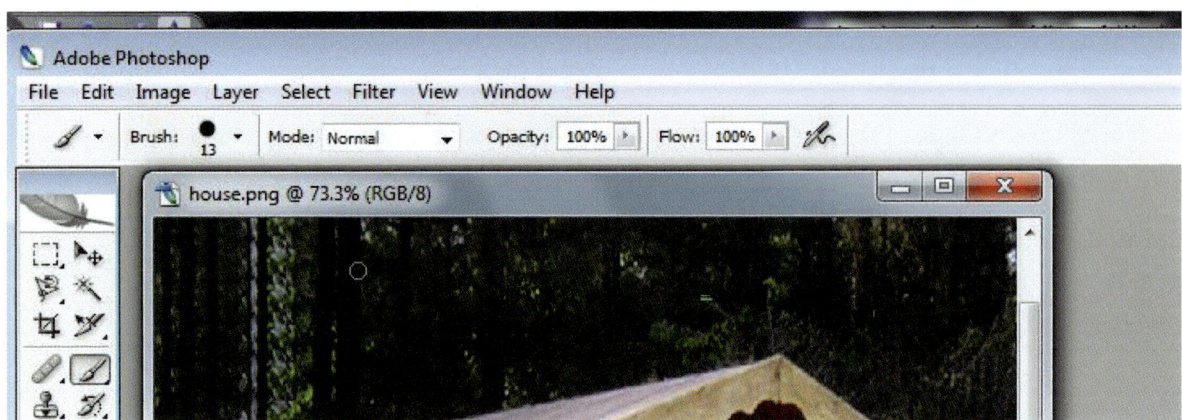

Palettes

The palettes open automatically with Photoshop and are useful for further refining the tools you will be using to modify your images.

In addition, the palettes are critical for working effectively with layers, as a navigation tool when you are retouching an image, and for correcting mistakes. These palettes can be closed and reopened depending on your Photoshop needs.

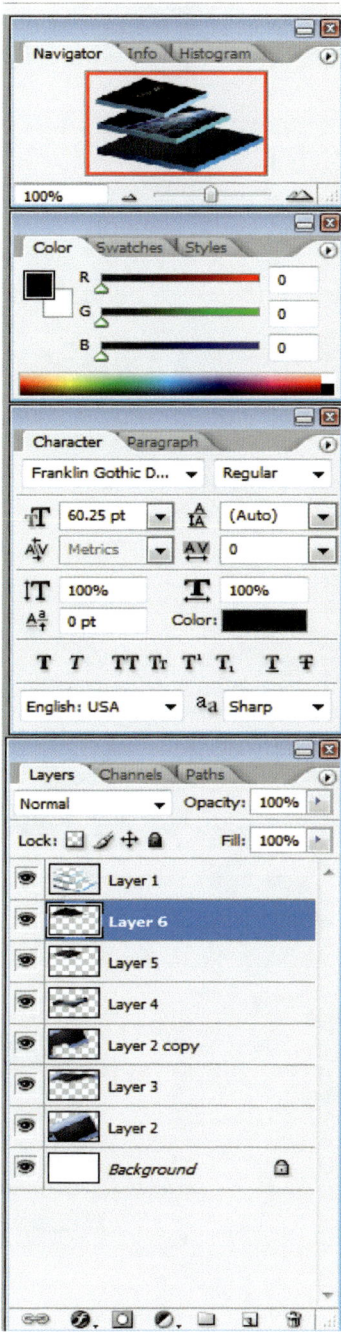

Importing Images

The first step in preparing to use Photoshop is to import a digital image. Although you can use Photoshop's drawing tools to create graphics from scratch.

There are a number of ways to obtain digital images:

> Scanners
> Digital cameras

Most of these can be found in the import menu

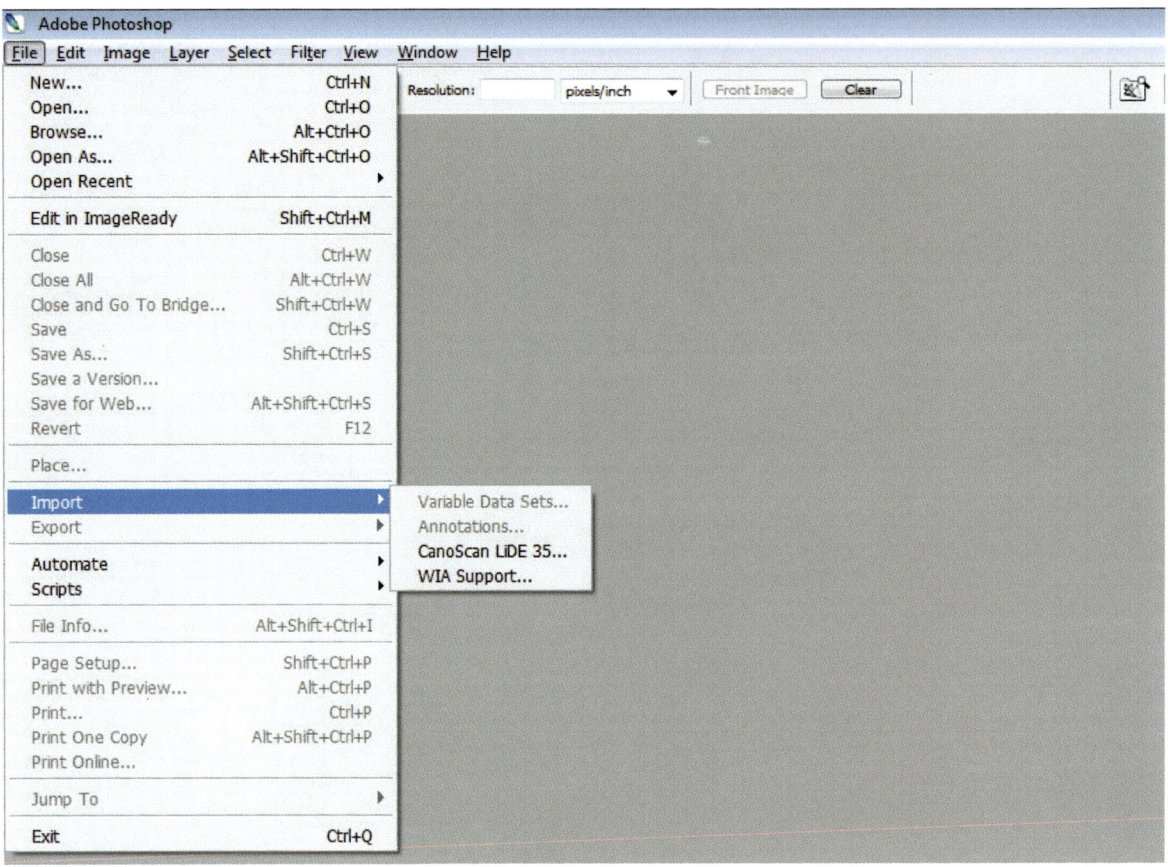

If you image already exists as a file then go to file -> open

Changing the Image Size

The Image Size menu allows you to view and adjust pixel information, document size and resolution in a single window.

The following example uses the Flower.jpg file in the Photoshop Resources folder.

Click on the Image menu and select Image Size. At the top of the window file size is displayed.

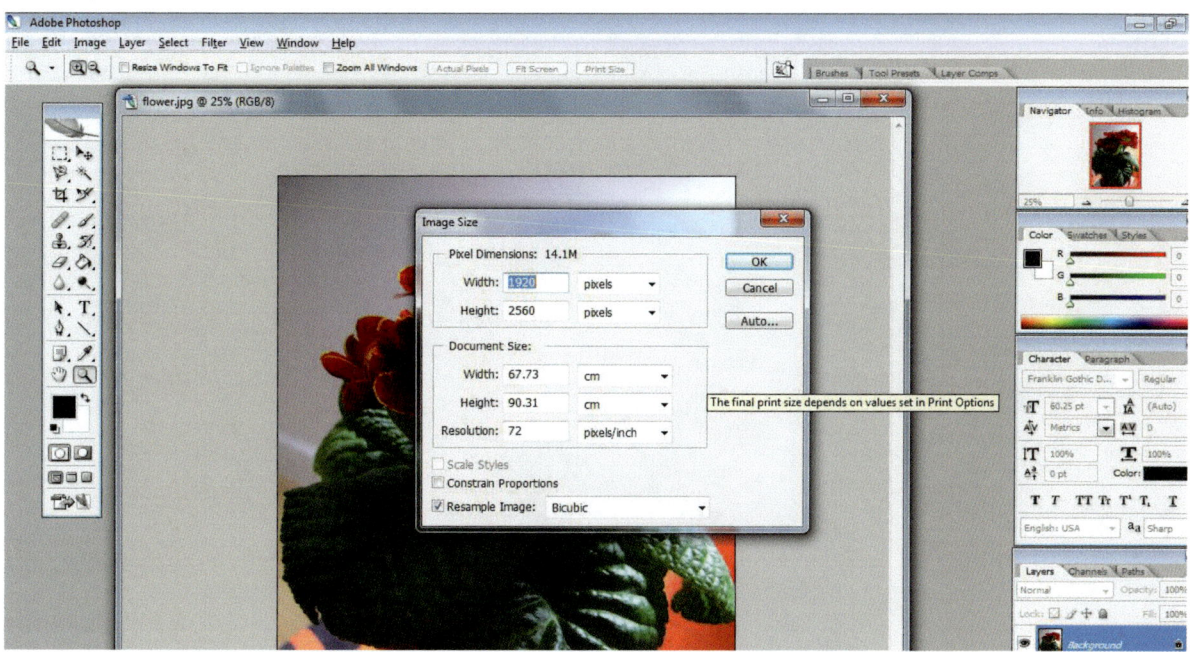

To adjust image size you can adjust the pixel dimensions in this window.

> This picture is 1920 pixels by 2560 pixels.

> Keeping the Constrain Proportions box checked allows you to change either the width or height of the image while maintaining the proportionate size of the picture.

If it's easier you can also change the picture size at a percentage by changing the pixels dropdown box to percentage

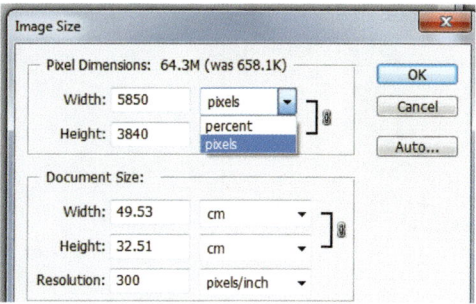

Rotate Canvas

Sometimes images are rotated because the camera was rotated when the picture was taken. It is easy to rotate and flip images in Photoshop.

Go to the Image menu and select Rotate Canvas.

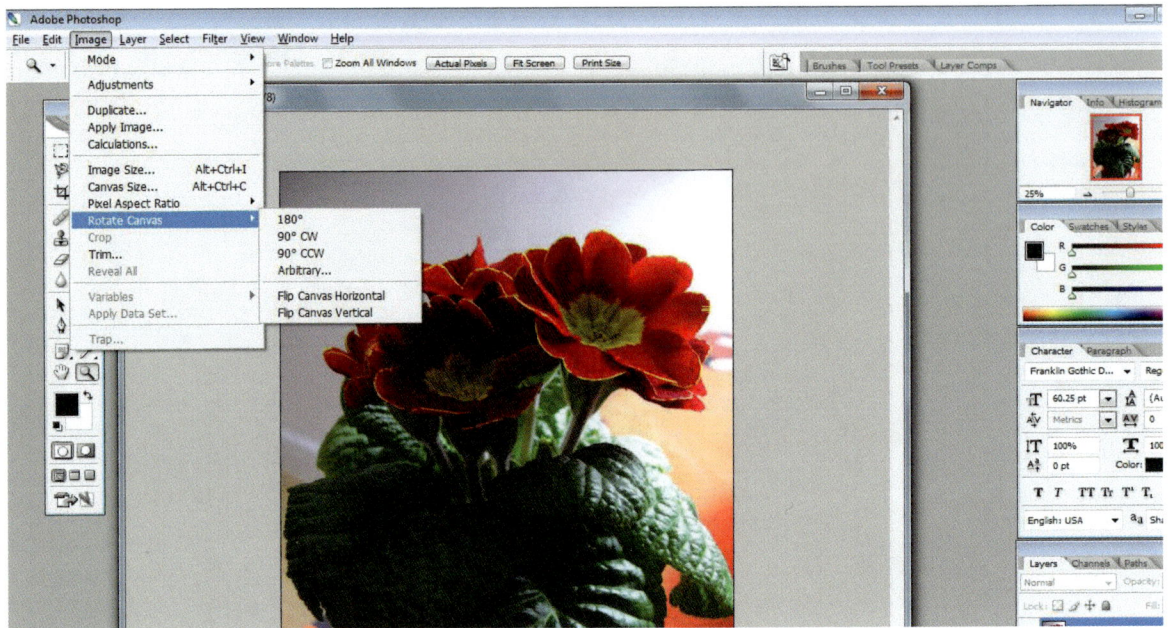

From the submenu, you have seven choices:

180° (rotates image 180°)

90° CW (Clockwise)

90° CCW (Anti-Clockwise)

Arbitrary – Let's you choose the angle, such as 45°.

Flip Horizontally   Flip Vertically

Cropping the Image

You can use the crop tool to crop an image as desired. This will can improve the appearance of your image, as well as decrease the file size.

For this example, we will use molly.jpg.

In the Toolbox, click on the Crop Tool.

Select the area you wish to keep by clicking and dragging a dotted line rectangle around the area. Notice how the area you want to keep is bright, but the area to be discarded is dimmed.

You can adjust the area you want to keep by clicking and dragging on the dotted lines.

Double-click in the centre of the highlighted area. This deletes and removes the area outside of the crop lines.

Adjusting the Image

Under the Image menu is a submenu called Adjustments. This menu provides us with a number of picture controls that can greatly improve the look and feel of our image.

To work with these tools, let's open another file called daffodils.jpg.

Go to the Image menu, select Adjustments, and then Auto Levels.

Photoshop now will do a standard calculation on the image to adjust the colour, contrast and balance. Auto levels changes the lightness and darkness of your colours, setting highlights and shadows.

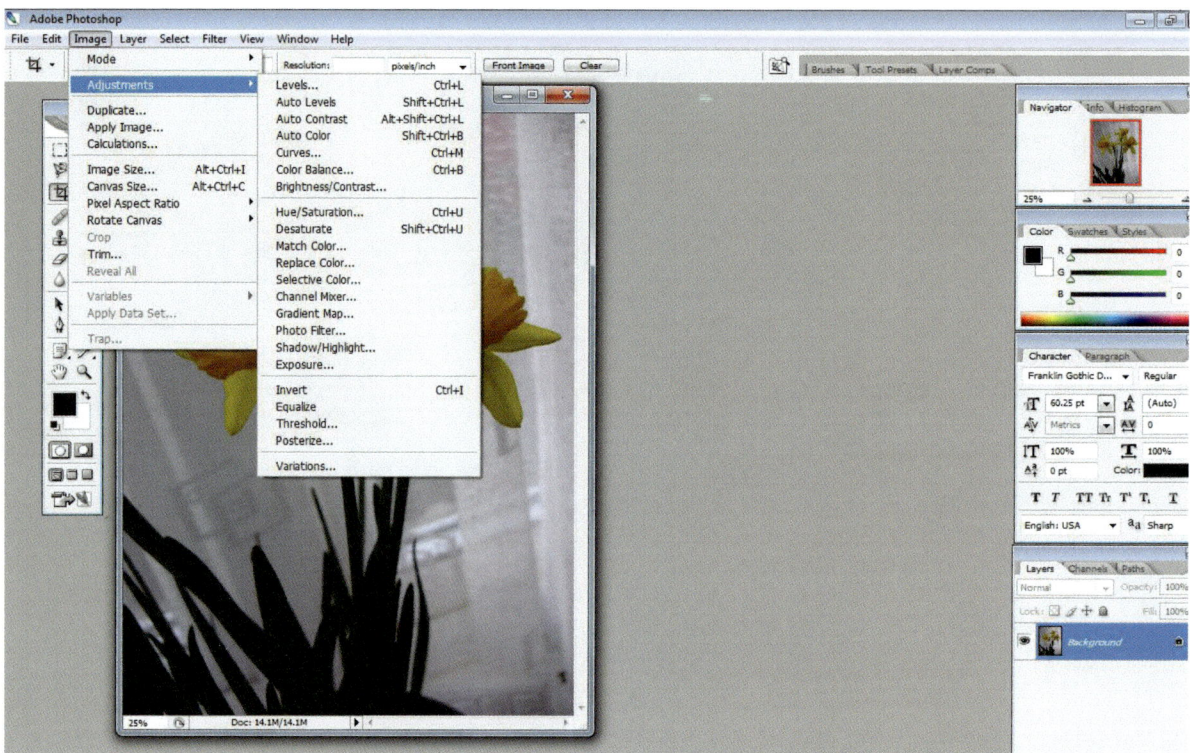

Hue/Saturation levels

We can also adjust the image using the Hue/Saturation levels, or Curves, which can adjust just the tint, intensity and brightness of your colours. An example of using this tool is to change the colour of flowers.

Open the daffodils.jpg image and save it as a Photoshop file in the working files folder.

Open the Hue/Saturation window under the Images/Adjustments menu

Move the slider left or right to change the hue of the image. Orange daffodils?

Brightness/Contrast

The Brightness/Contrast tool is extremely useful for making adjustments to the lighting where using Auto levels is ineffective.

Open the brighton.jpg image.

Go to Image/Adjustments/ and select Brightness/Contrast.

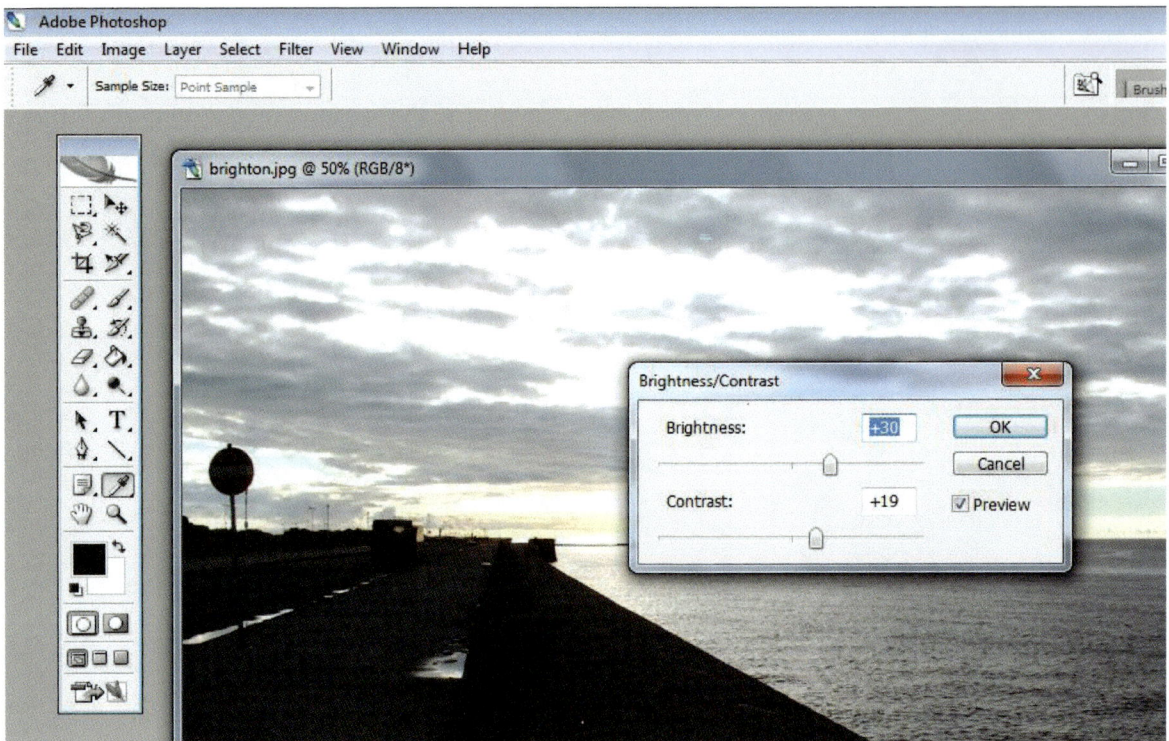

Move the Brightness slider to the right to lighten the picture.

Move the Contrast slider to the right to add back some of the picture's detail.

Shadows & Highlights

There is actually another way to adjust picture brightness that may work better for photos with underexposed areas. Under the Image/Adjustments menu is a menu called Shadows/Highlights. This menu provides us a control to lighten areas that are dark due to shadows. A second control lets us add back some highlights by darkening part of the picture.

To work with these tools, let's open brighton.jpg.

Go to the Image menu, select Adjustments, and then Shadows/Highlights. Photoshop now will open a window and make an initial setting to reduce shadows by 50%.

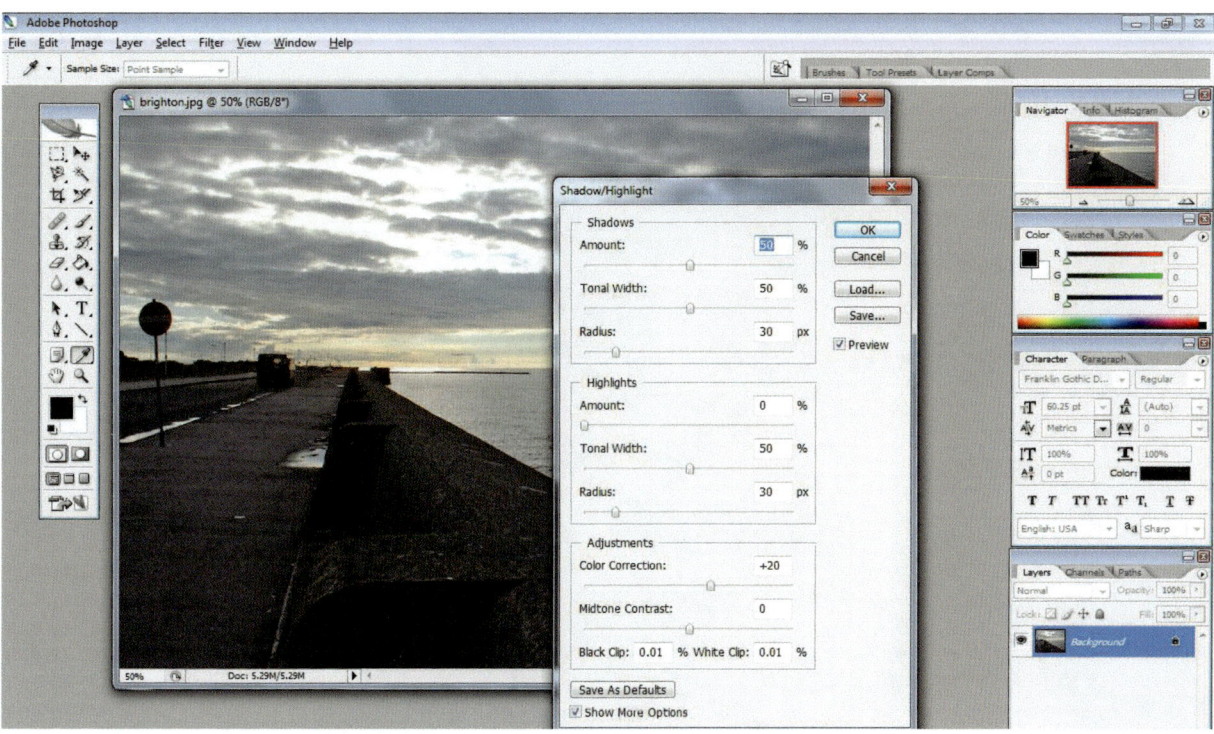

We can change the amount of shadow by moving the slider left or right. Moving the slider completely to the right removes 100% (as Photoshop calculates) of the shadows. Notice the additional detail on the road. At the same time, the sky remains cloudy, rather than being bright and washed out as when only using the Brightness control.

The Highlight control allows us to bring out some of the detail in the surrounding picture without darkening the area too much. Use this control sparingly.

Touching up the Image

Dodge Tool

Tools such as the Dodge can be used to lighten a dark, undefined area of a picture to bring out the detail.

Open the house.png image and use the Dodge Tool to lighten the path in the lower front left of the picture.

Burn Tool

The burn tool can be used to darken an area.

Click and hold the cursor on the Dodge Tool in the ToolBox. A short submenu with three options pops up. Select the Burn Tool.

In the house.png image and use the Burn Tool to darken the trees in the background to make the cabin stand out more.

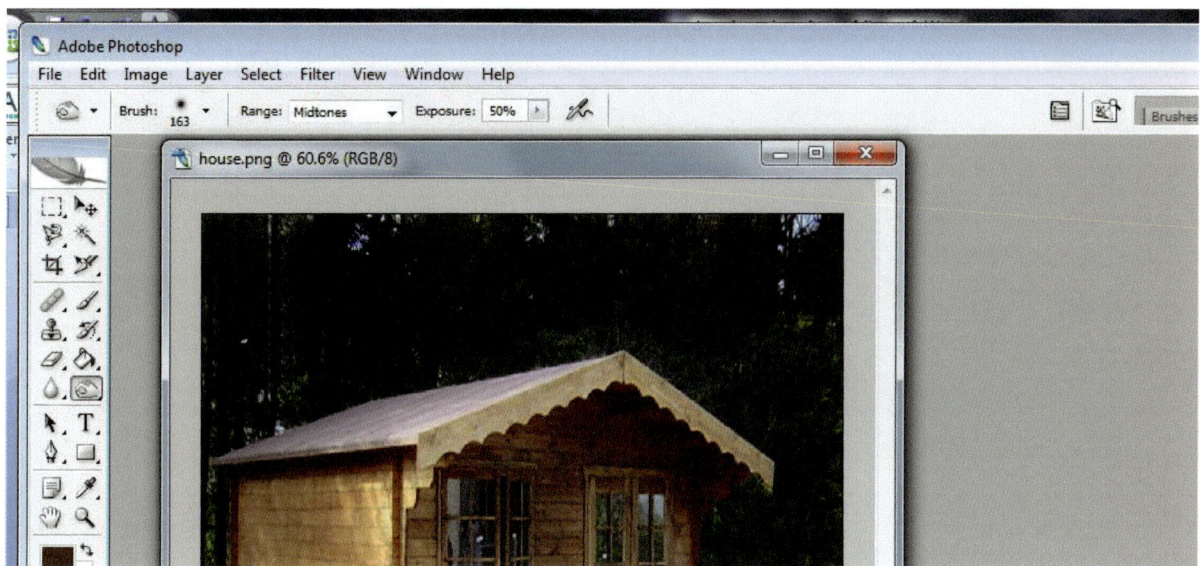

Heal Tool

Another useful tool is the Heal Tool. This tool uses information in an area that you select to replace another area of the image. For our example we will use an old photograph that has been damaged.

Open the oldimage.jpg image

Select the Heal Tool from the tool box. (It is grouped with the Color Replacement tool.)

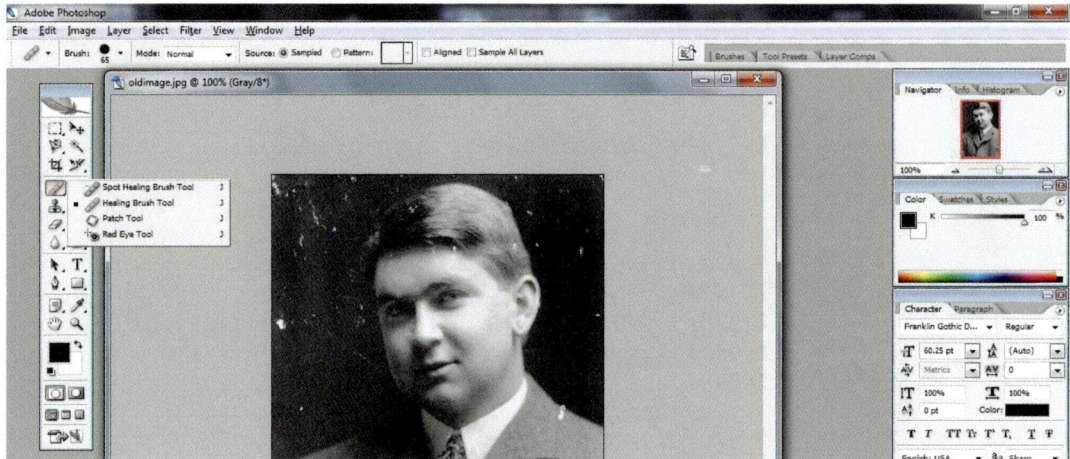

Alt or Option-Click on an area that is good and can be used to as a "donor" to "heal" another area.

Now click on the area to be repaired.

Continue clicking on areas to be repaired, selecting new "donor" areas as the content of the image changes.

Magnetic Lasso Tool

Sometimes it is necessary to remove an object from an image. This is useful if you want the object and not the background. We can do this with the magnetic lasso, it is possible to replace the background to that it appears that the unwanted object never existed in the image.

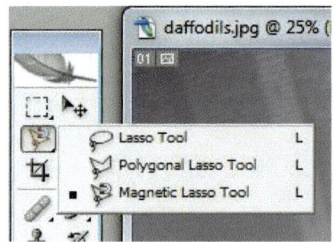

Open the daffodils.jpg image.

Use the Magnetic Lasso to select the daffodils in the photo.

Now trace around the daffodils with the lasso, you will find that it will magnetically stick to the edge of the yellow flower. If it doesn't then click your mouse to manually add a point.

You can now copy and paste this Edit -> Copy; Edit -> Paste

Clone Stamp tool.

Sometimes it is necessary to remove an object from a photograph. We can do this with the Clone Stamp tool.

Open the brightonlight.jpg image.

Start there to paint in the same pattern as you just selected. I want to get rid of the street sign in the image. Hold down ALT or OPTION on your keyboard and click an area close to the sign. This is the area we want to clone.

Paint over the sign a click at a time until the sign disappears.

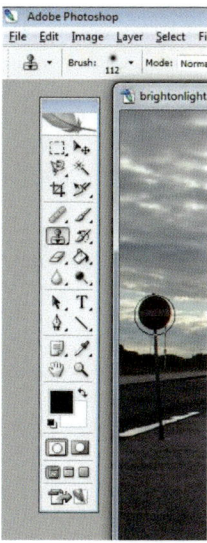 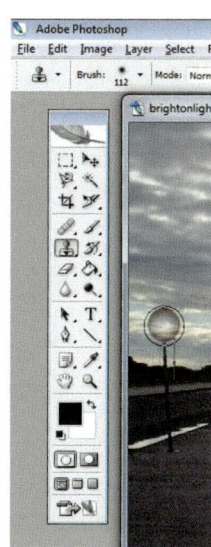 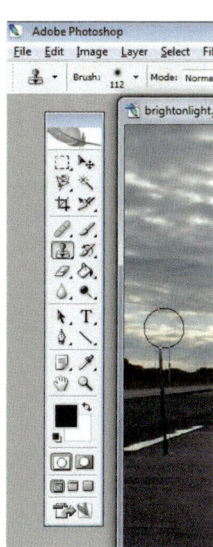

Select different spots so that you don't repeat too much of an area.

Do the same with the sign's pole, this is a bit trickier as you have to clone the intricate details of the road. Use the same technique as above do a small edge next to the pole and clone.

Using Layers

When you first open a photo, there is generally only a background layer.

We add layers (like transparency sheets) to create our effects.

Layer effects are NOT applied to the 'background' layer by default.

However, you can turn the background into a layer in order to make more Photoshop effects available.

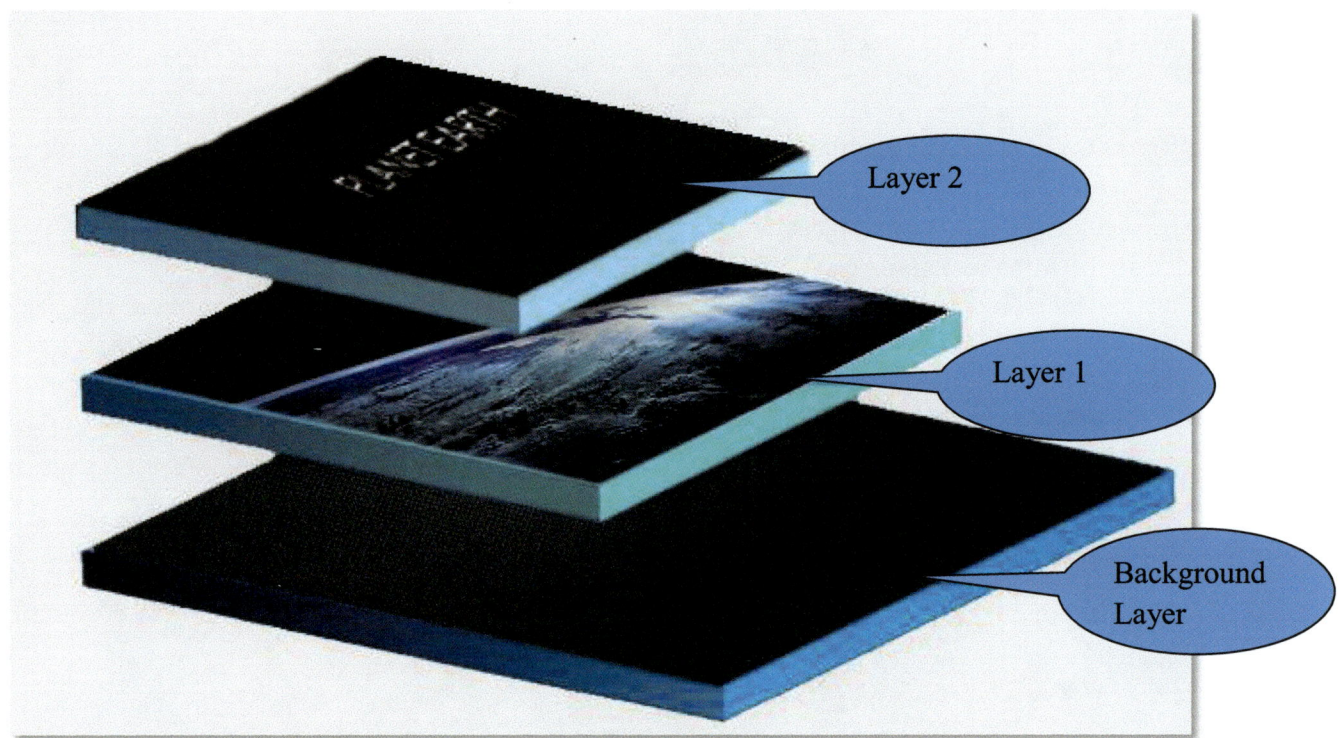

Creating a Collage of Images

Using Layer Opacity and Feathering to create a collage.

Now the open the house.png image. Using the Magnetic Lasso Tool make a selection around the cabin.

When you close the loop you will see animated dotted lines (marching ants) around your selection. Go to Select > Feather and make the feather radius 2 pixels.

Go to Edit > Copy. Now load up lake.psd then go to Edit > Paste. The cabin will appear on a new layer titled "Layer 1"

With Layer 1 still highlighted, go to Edit > Transform > Scale and reduce the image to about 1/3 its original size or until it fits nicely. Now click out of the transform and select Apply. Using the Move Tool place this image where you like it.

Use the Move Tool to move this selection so that its bottom end touches the "ground" in the lake image.

A challenge for you. Notice in the windows on the cabin door, you can see some of the original image. See if you can remove that to show the scene of the lake through the window

Marquee Selection & Free Transform

Using the Transform & Scale with Layer Styles it is possible to create a map with a zoom-effect.

Open the file "moon.png"

Using the marquee tool select the moon.

Copy this selection by going to Edit > Copy

Open up "planetearth.psd"

Then paste (Edit > Paste) it as a new layer. Make sure image you pasted in is behind the earth. Do this by dragging 'Layer 1' below 'Earth' in the layers pallet bottom right.

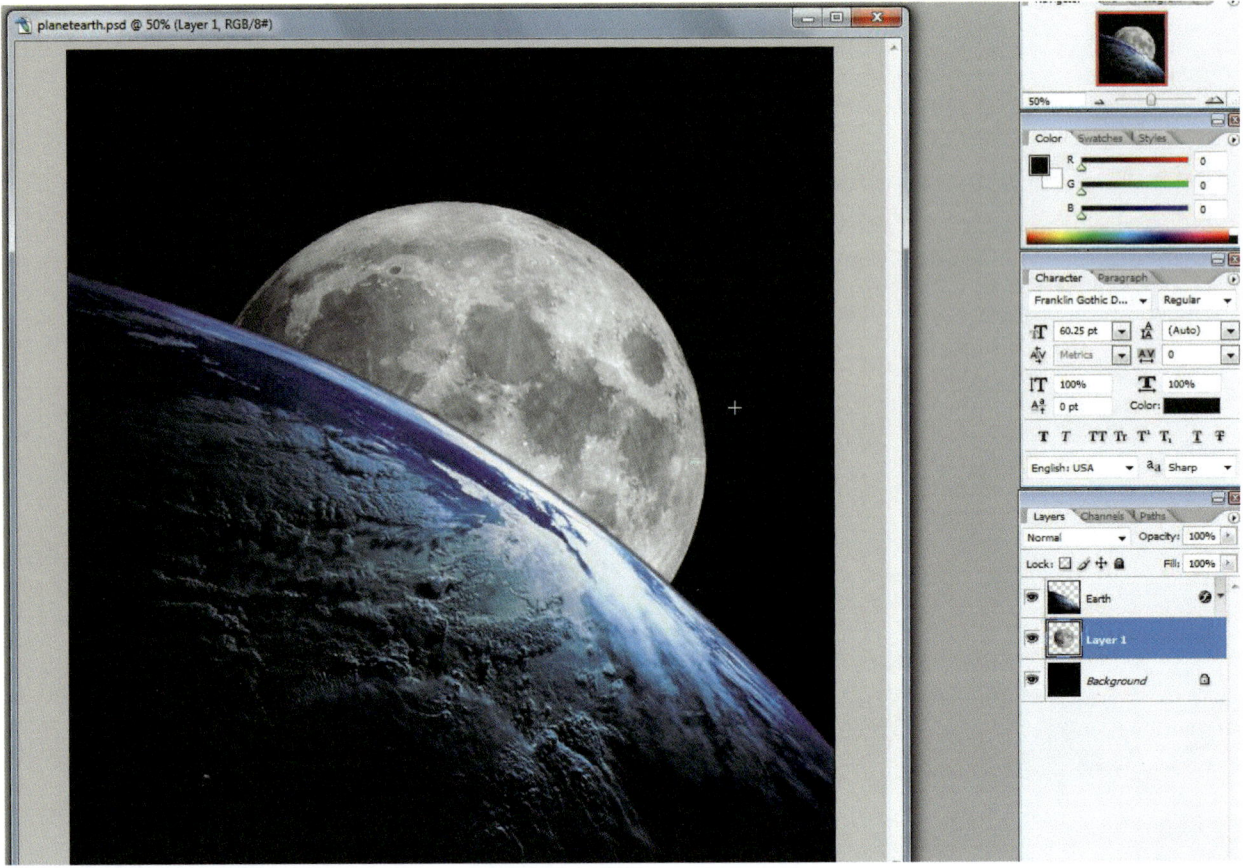

With "Layer 1" selected go to Edit > Transform > Scale.

Drag the selectors so that the moon seems smaller than the earth. When you're satisfied, select any other tool (to deactivate the transform) and select Apply.

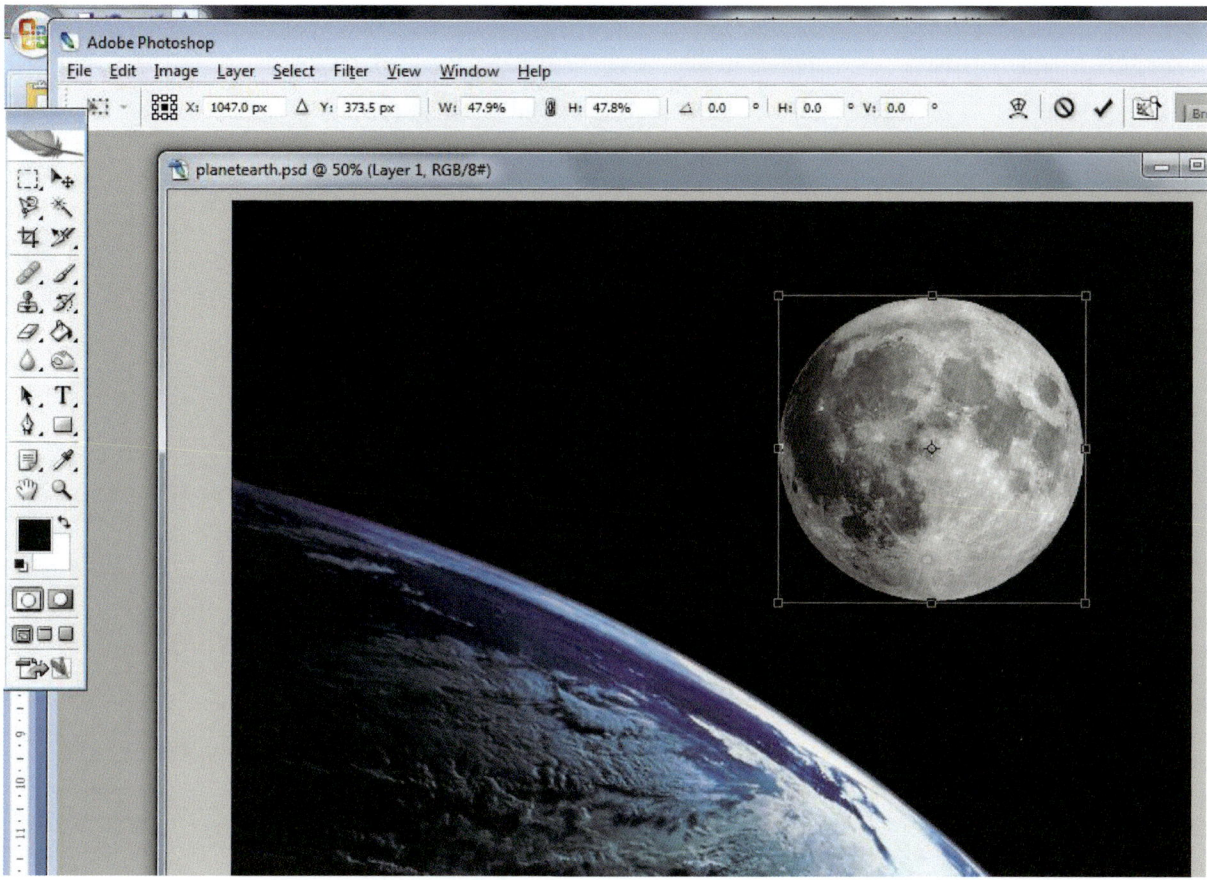

Layer Styles

Carrying on from the last section, if not, open the file planetearth.psd

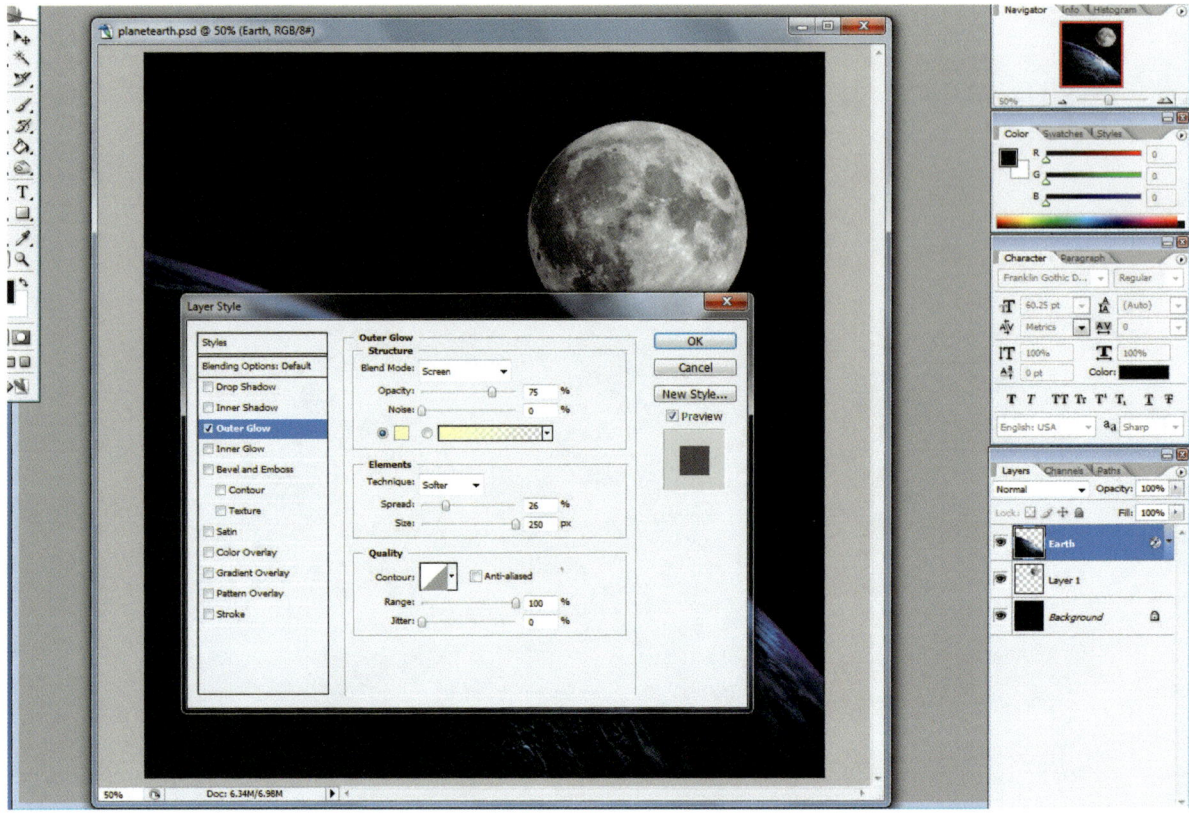

Double click on the Earth layer in the layers pallet to bring up Layer Style

Click Outer Glow.

Change the Spread to a value of 50% and the Size to a value of 160 px.

Adding Text

Let's use some text to title our image. Photoshop uses vector mapping to create text. You can use the Text Tool to add text with the font, size, and other features desired.

Carrying on from the last section, if not, open planetearth.psd

Click on the Text Tool in your toolbox.

Select a nice font , size and colour (3d81ff) in the bar below

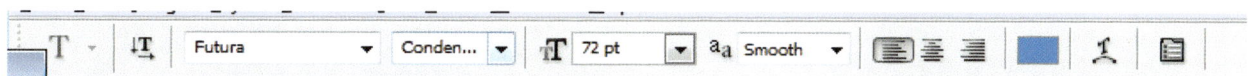

Click on the image where you want to place the text.

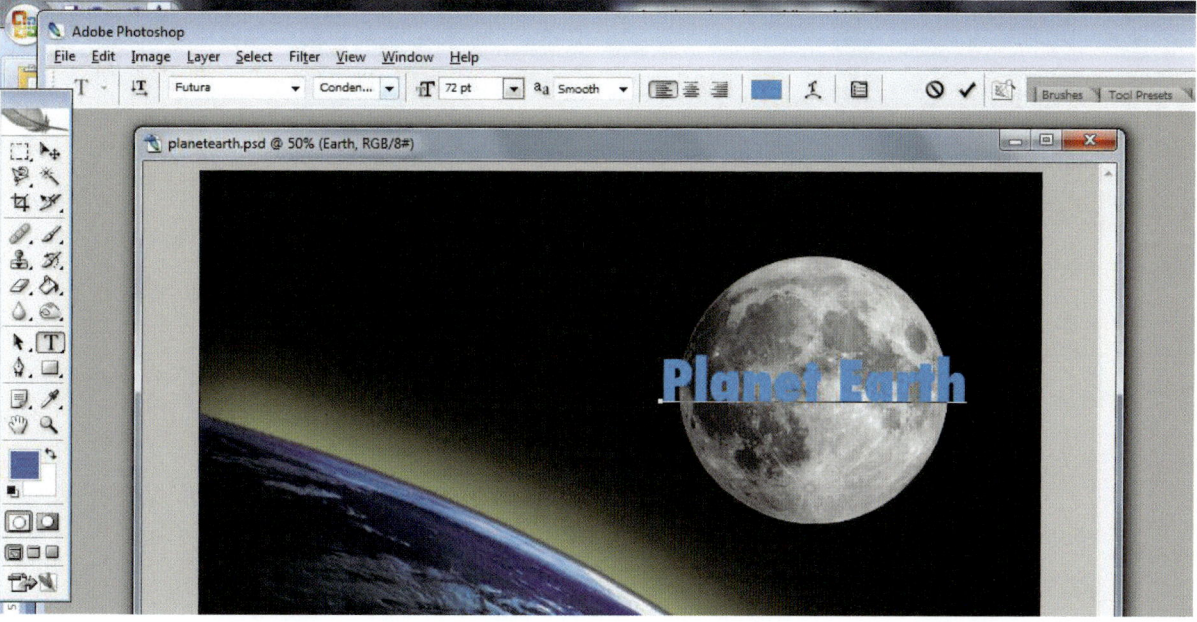

Type in a title.

Double click on the text layer in the layers pallet to bring up a menu for special effects. Click 'Bevel and Emboss".

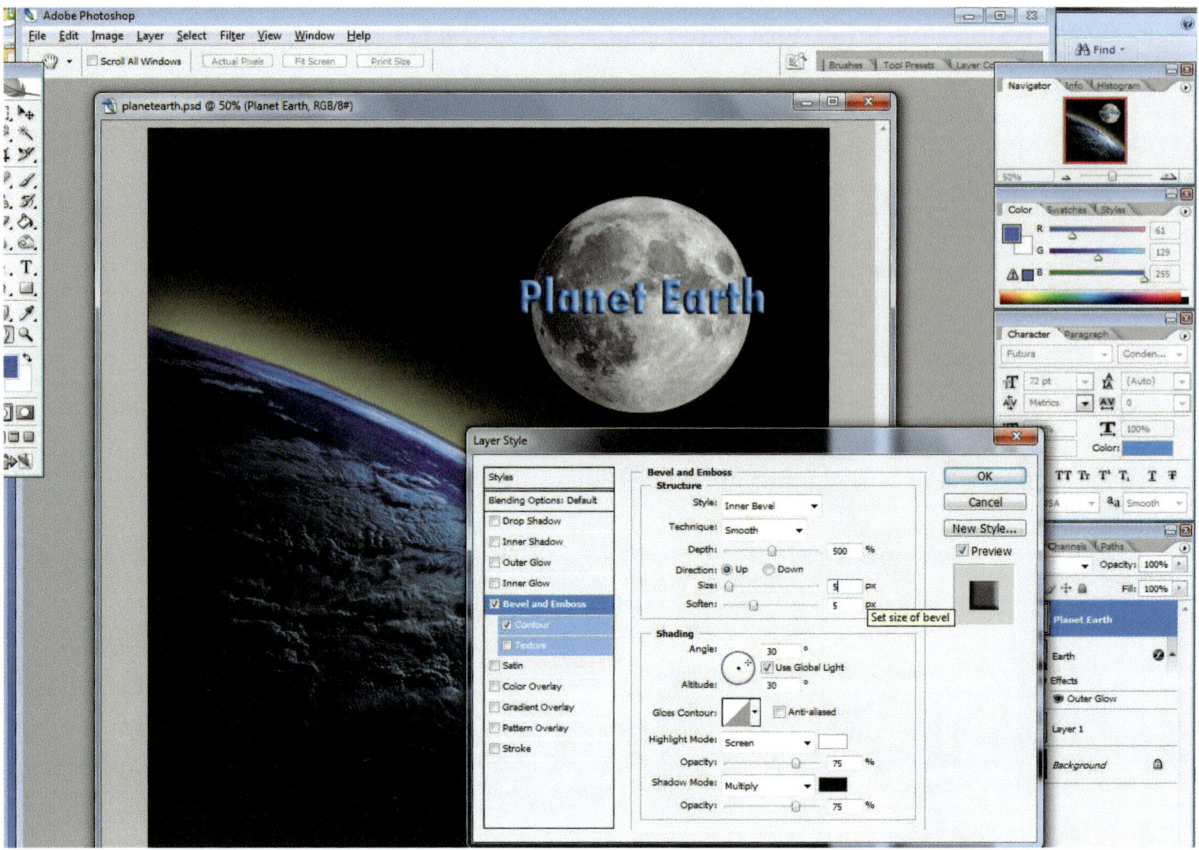

Now we can move this text to wherever we want. From the toolbox select the Move Tool.

Try experimenting with different effects. How about a nice outer glow?

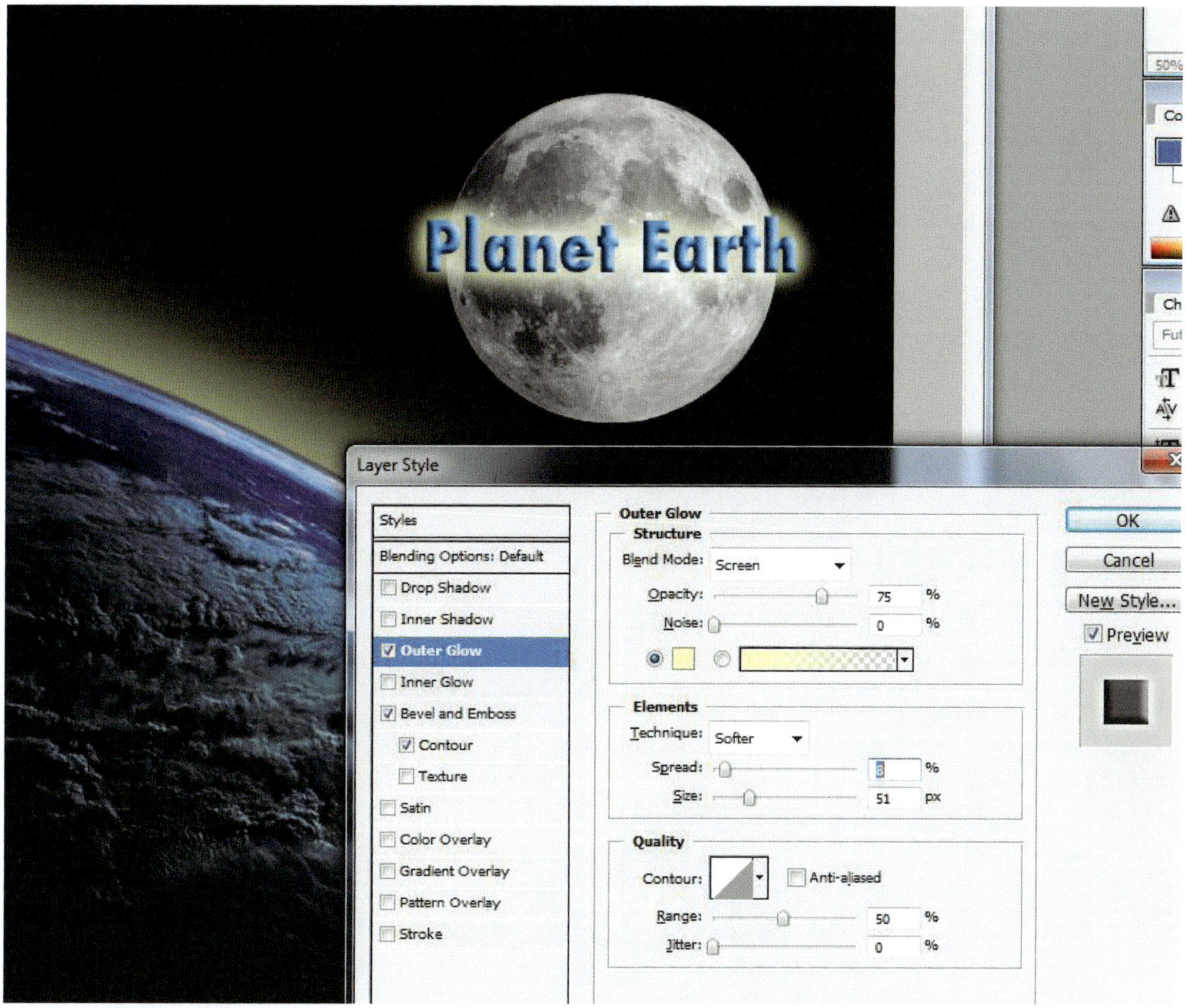

Layer Style		

Styles

Blending Options: Default
☐ Drop Shadow
☐ Inner Shadow
☑ Outer Glow
☐ Inner Glow
☑ Bevel and Emboss
   ☑ Contour
   ☐ Texture
☐ Satin
☐ Color Overlay
☐ Gradient Overlay
☐ Pattern Overlay
☐ Stroke

Outer Glow
Structure

Blend Mode: Screen
Opacity: 75 %
Noise: 0 %

Elements
Technique: Softer
Spread: 8 %
Size: 51 px

Quality
Contour: ☐ Anti-aliased
Range: 50 %
Jitter: 0 %

OK
Cancel
New Style...
☑ Preview

To adjust the position of this text, place the Move Tool on your text, click and drag it to the correct location.

41

Special Effects

Filters

Photoshop has a large number of Filters that will convert your image when applied and give it a special look or characteristic. Filters range from those that apply a particular painting effect to those that imitate different camera settings.

Some of the more practical of these tools are the

Sharpen/Sharpen filter (which helps sharpen up the edges of a slightly blurry image);

Blur/Gaussian Blur (which can be used to create soft edges on an image);

Noise/Dust & Scratches (which is useful for making corrections to damaged photographs)

Radial Blur

Open the carwindow.jpg image. Select radial blur. The entire image now looks like the car is moving really fast.

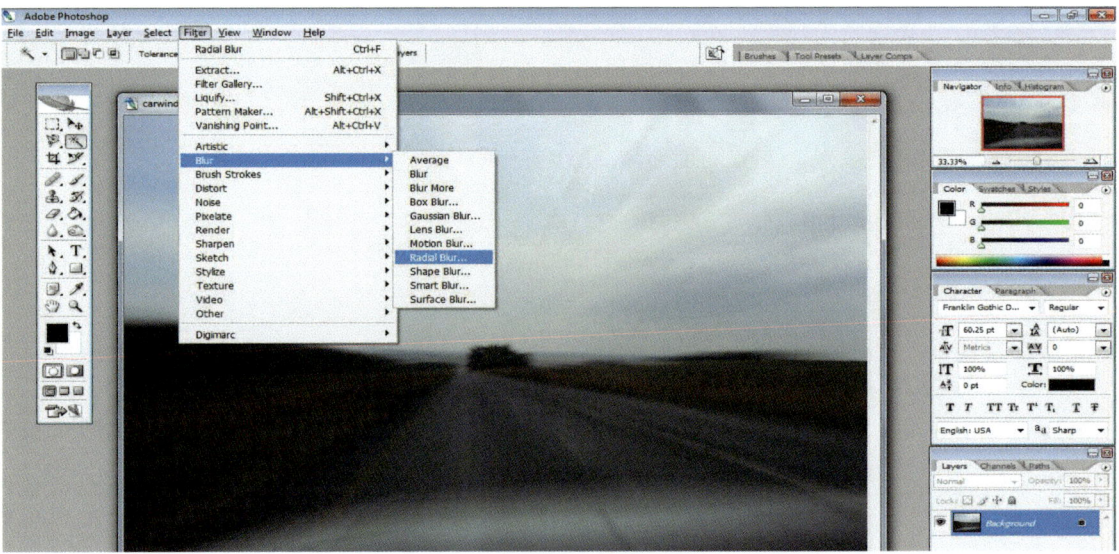

The easiest way to experiment with the filters is to open the Filter Gallery and try them one at a time.

Lighting Effects

Photoshop has a large number of filers that allow you to add certain effects to your images to give them a special look.

Open house.png image and from the filter menu click render then lighting effects.

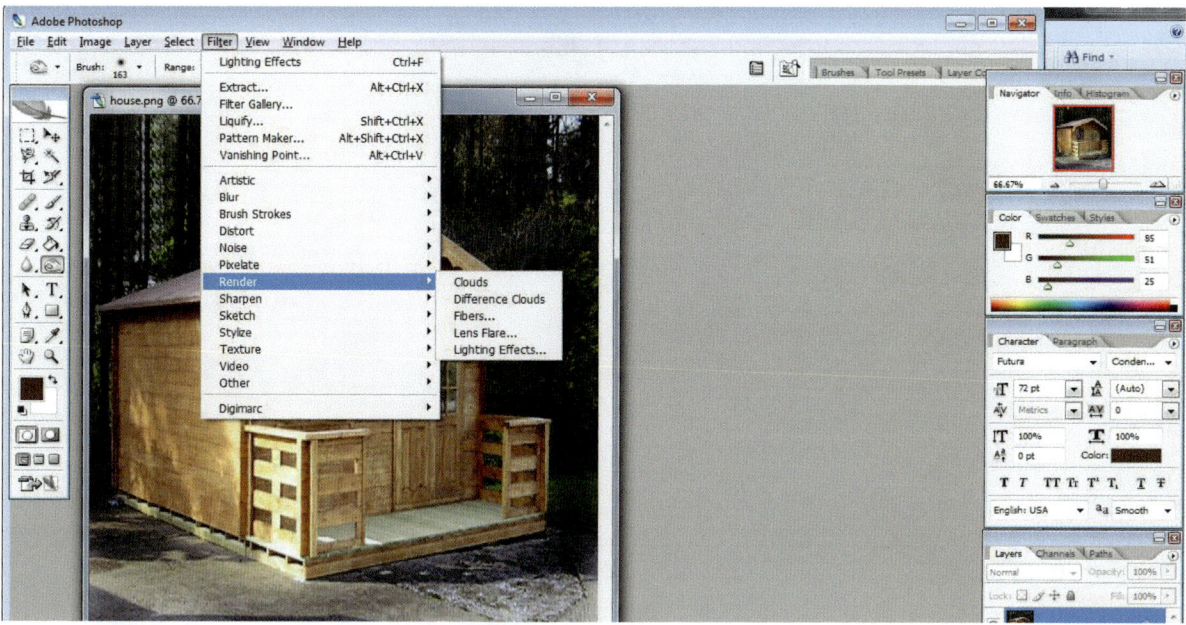

From the lighting effects box you can choose a number of different types of lights, and adjust the intensity, direction and focus. Try experimenting with different light settings.

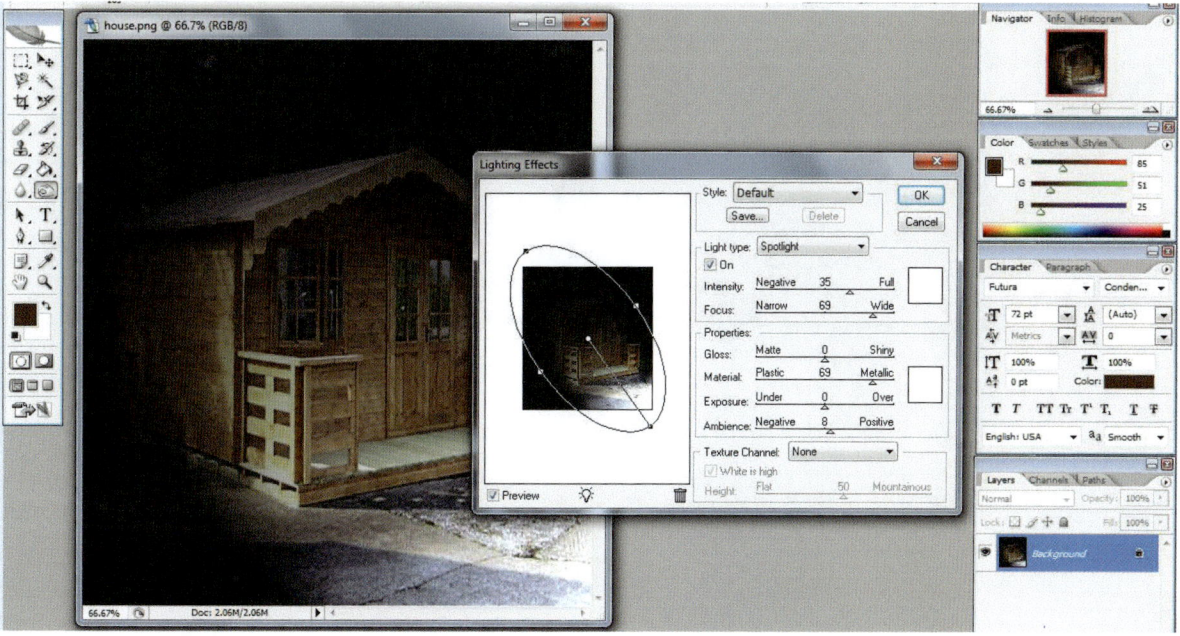

You can also use lighting effects to or correct for lighting. Try this with window.psd

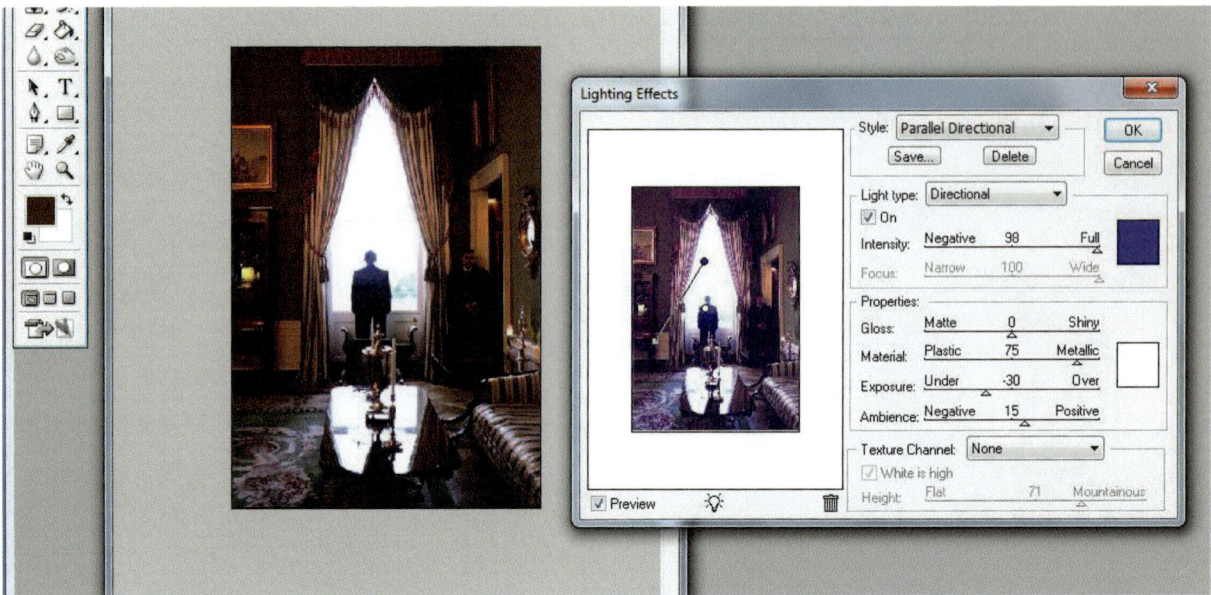

Or to add atmosphere to photographs. Change the light type to directional, drag the line to the window, this is where you want the light to point from.

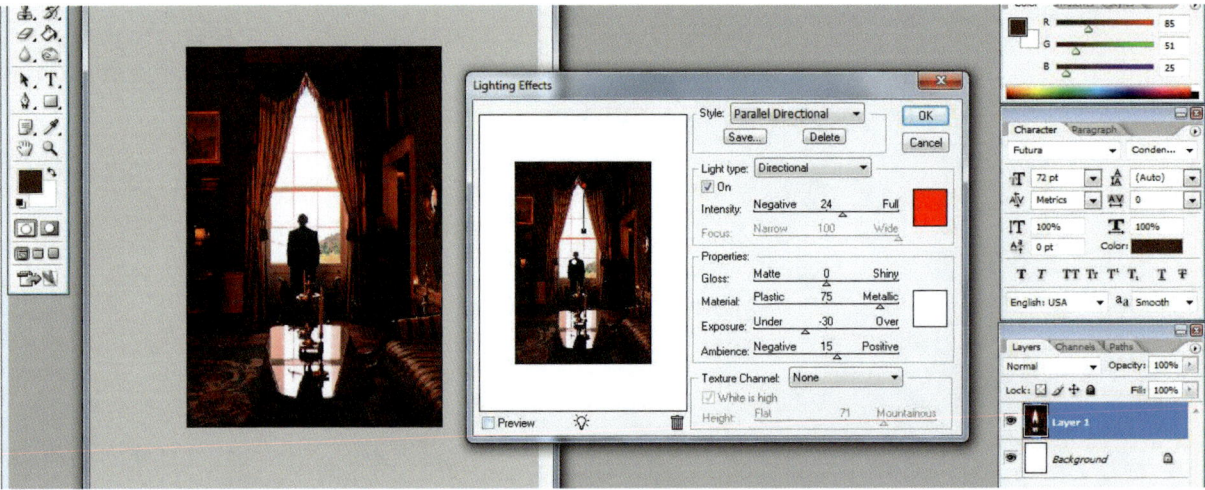

Combining Photos for Special Effects

You can use the selection tools and the 'Paste Into' command to create interesting special effects. In the example below, lightening will be added behind windows in a second photo to give the effect that the there is a storm inside a building.

Open the lightning.jpg image.

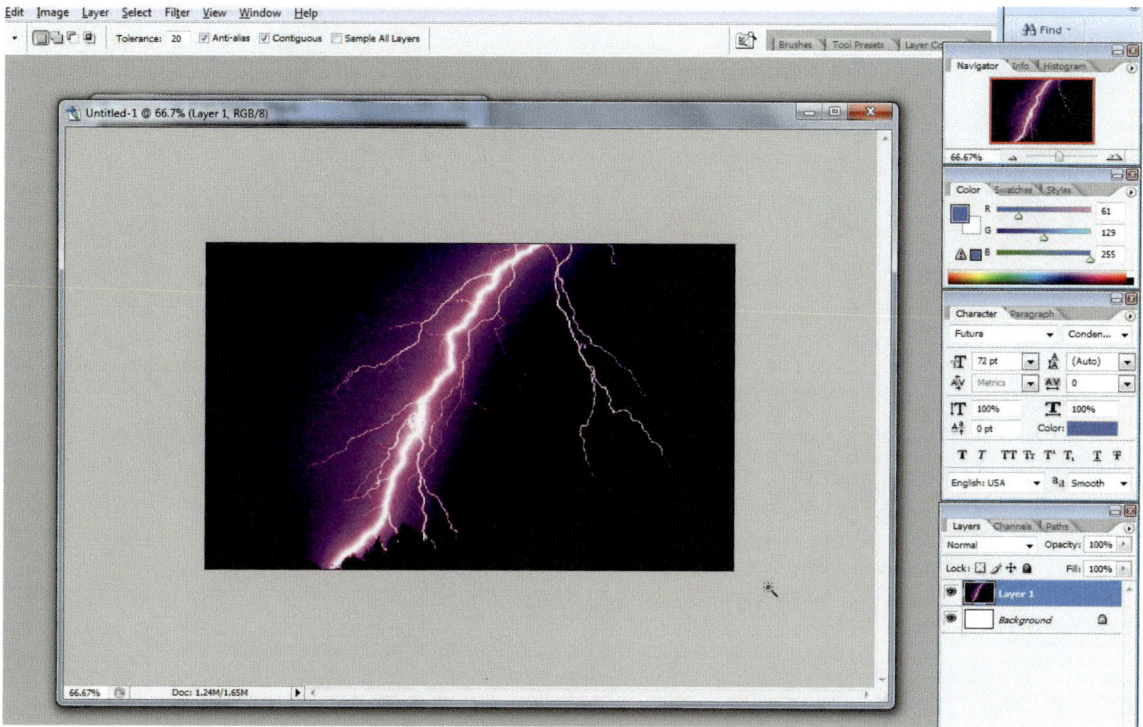

Use the Brightness/Contrast menu to adjust the image if desired.

Use either the Select/All command to select the entire image, or the Rectangle Marquee tool to select the image.

Then use Edit/Copy to copy the selection to the clipboard.

Open the windows.png image.

Using the rectangular marquee tool, start in one of the square window panes and select the interior of the pane. Make sure that the Style of the Marquee tool is set to Normal in the Options bar.

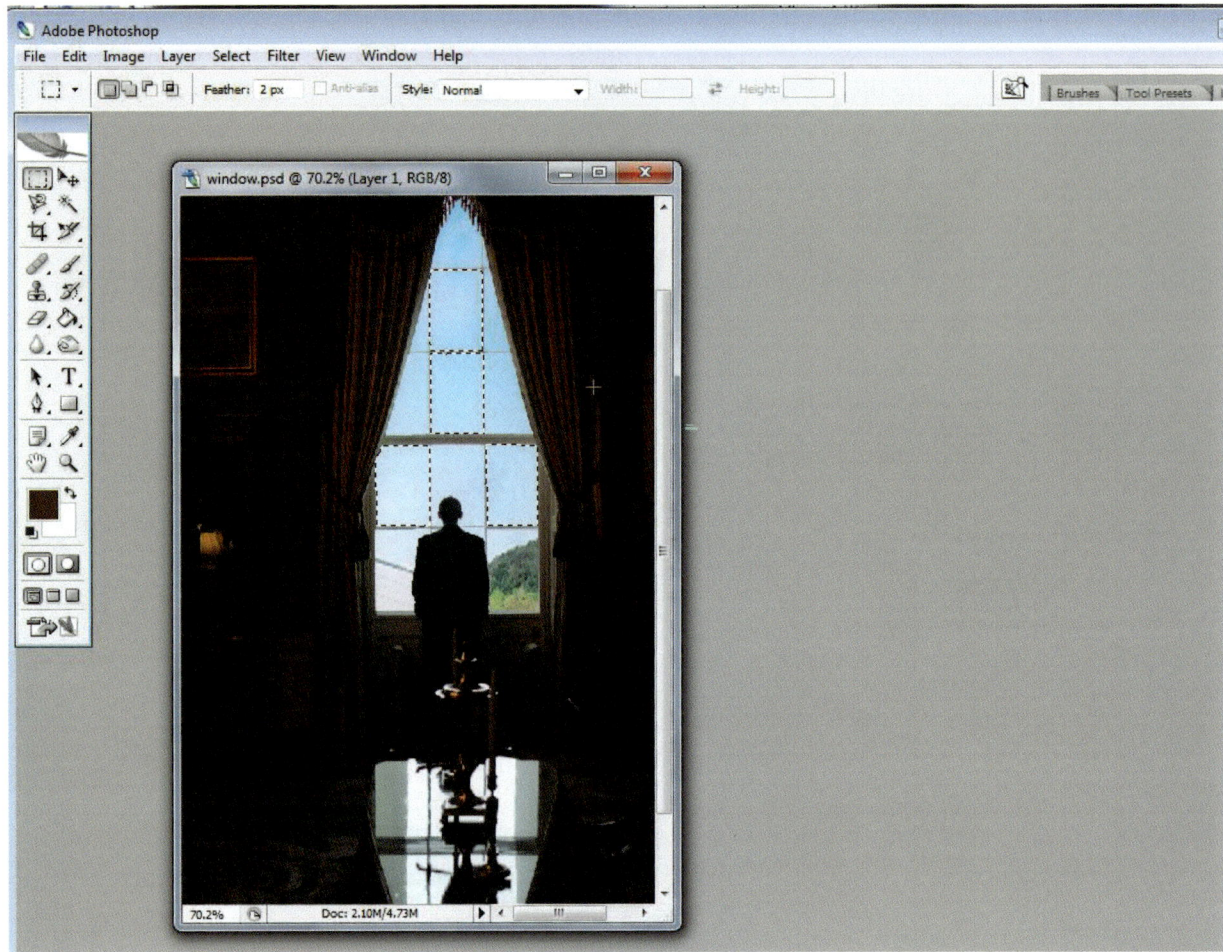

Now, you can add to this selection by holding down the shift key so that you can continue selecting just the interior panes (leaving the window frames).

Now still holding the shift key, select the magnetic lasso tool to select the triangular shapes at the top of the window.

Once all the shapes are selected, go to the Edit menu and select the 'Paste Into' command.

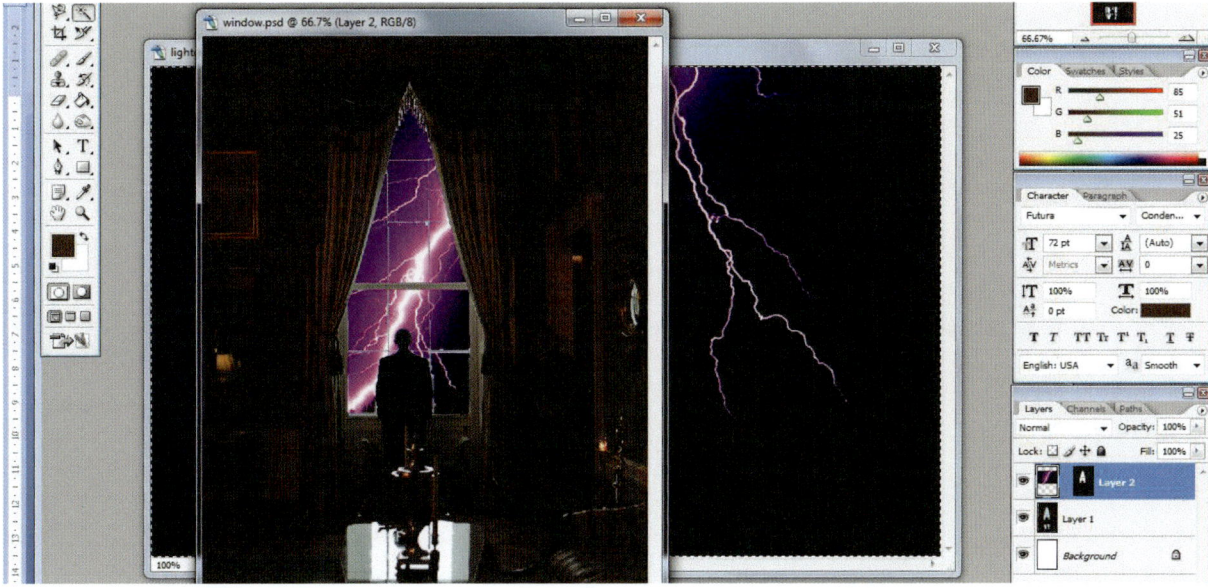

This will cut the selected panes and paste behind it the selection we made earlier from the lightning picture. The Paste Into command pastes the lightning selection BEHIND the window panes that we cut out.

Now go to the Move tool, and you can move the lightning picture around until you like the effect in the windows. The window picture has effectively become a mask for the lightning picture which lies behind it.

A challenge for you. You might also notice there is a reflection on the table, see if you can create a reflection of the lightening storm on the table to match the one seen though the window.

Appendix

File Formats

Once we scan the image at the desired size and resolution, it is important to save the image before beginning to work on it. How we save will determine how much flexibility we ultimately have with the image. Which format we use will also affect file size.

Understanding the variety of digital file formats available to us can help us select the best format for our needs. Although there are many different kinds of digital image file formats, each with their own capabilities and restrictions, here is a brief summary of the most common formats.

TIFF "Tagged Image File Format", most common cross platform format for images. Virtually all paint, image editing and page layout applications support this format.

PICT Apple's proprietary image format

GIF "Graphic Interchange Format" - popular Web graphic format limited to 8-bit images (256 colours).

JPEG "Joint Photographic Experts Group" - also popular Web graphic format

EPS "Encapsulated PostScript file" - used by programs such as PageMaker and Illustrator.

Photoshop PSD Adobe's own file format, with the extension .psd

PNG A new format developed as a patent-free alternative to GIF for lossless compression supporting 24-bit images (16.7 million colours).

One of the major differences between these various formats is the method of file compression. Compression attempts to make the files smaller while retaining the integrity of the image. Formats do this to varying degrees of success, depending on the type of image, and the type of compression used.

There are two basic types of compression, "lossy" and "lossless".

Lossy loses pixel information from the original file.

Lossless retains all the pixel information, regardless of how often you save the file.

This is important to us because the two basic types of formats we use on the web, "gif" and "jpeg" are very different. Gifs do not use compression, but can only display 256 colours. This is not a good format for photographs. However, jpegs, which are wonderful for true colour image quality, use lossy compression, which degrades the image when you save it.

Whether we ultimately save our images as .gif, .jpg or .png depending on its final use, we do not want to work with this format in Photoshop.

When working with images, it's recommend to work on your high resolution master images.

First, keeping these considerations in mind save all scanned images at a relatively high resolution in the .tiff format in a folder called master.

Then make a copy of these images to work with for the project (in a working files folder), saving your work as Photoshop files (which preserves your layers).

The final images should be saved in the appropriate format (.gif or .jpeg, etc.) in a folder called images for the project. This way insures that you will always have your scanned originals available for future use or if you need to make changes.

Digital Images

Photoshop works with bitmap images. This uses thousands of pixels to represent the image. Each pixel (the smallest, basic unit of a digital image and the dots of light on a computer monitor) has a value, which specifies its colour and location. When you work with bitmap images, you are editing pixels, rather than shapes. This allows for gradations of colour and creating a continuous tone appearance.

However, because bitmap images contain a fixed number of pixels, they can lose detail or appear jagged edged when they are rescaled on the screen or printed at a higher resolution than they were created for.

A vector graphic, on the other hand, is made up of lines and curves defined by mathematical formulas. Because of this, you can move, resize or change the colour of the graphic without losing image quality. This type of graphic is the best choice when you want a logo or bold graphic.

Resolution

Understanding how pixel data is measured and displayed will help you make decisions about your images both when scanning and working with the images in Photoshop.

Pixel Dimensions: How large an image displays on the computer screen is determined by the pixel dimensions of the image plus the size and setting of the monitor.

On a typical 15" monitor set to 800x600, an 800x600 image would fill the screen. This same image would fill the screen of a 19" inch monitor if it were also set to 800x600; each pixel on the 19" screen would be larger.

Likewise, if the 19" monitor were set to 1024x768, the image would appear much smaller.

Image Resolution: the number of pixels in an image, which determines the quality and detail of that image. Image resolution controls how much space these pixels are spread over when printed. For printing, a high resolution image contains more and therefore smaller pixels than an image with a low resolution. This means that a 1 inch by 1 inch image at 72 dpi would have 5184 pixels, whereas the same image at 300 dpi would have 90,000 pixels. A higher resolution image produces more detail and subtler colour transitions. However, increasing the resolution of an image only spreads the original pixel information over a larger number of pixels and will not improve image quality.

Monitor Resolution: Most new monitors today have a resolution of 96 dpi – dots per inch (older Macintosh monitors only had a resolution of 72 dpi). No matter how high the resolution may be we cannot see more than 96 pixels/inch in the displayed picture on a computer. When the resolution of the image matches that of the output device, we cannot see the individual elements that make up the image and the image appears continuous to the eye.

Printer Resolution: The number of pixels in a given image also translates somewhat to the resolution on a printer, commonly referred to as dpi (dots per inch). Printers vary widely, from 300 dpi available on older laser writers, to 4800 dpi for some of the newer inkjet printers. As a general rule your image resolution should be double that of the resolution used to print the image.

Note about colour: A computer screen delivers colour in an RGB format, meaning it combines red, green and blue. Printers on the other hand, are generally described by the colours cyan, magenta, yellow and black, or CMYK. Matching colours that you see on the screen with what gets printed on a given printer, is a constant source of exasperation for many.

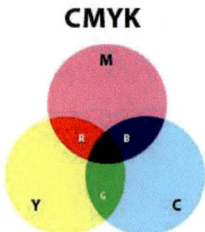

Image size

Is my Picture 350k or 125MB?

We now know that resolution describes how many pixels we have in a given image, and the number of pixels determines how much information can be displayed, or how good the picture looks. This quantity of pixels also determines how large our file will be.

100 dpi   200 dpi   300 dpi

400 dpi   500 dpi   600 dpi

A 2.6" x 3" image translates to:

> 72 dpi - 128k
> 150 dpi - 508k
> 300 dpi - 1.97mb
> 600 dpi - 7.89mb
> 1200 dpi - 31.6mb

Although selecting too low a resolution can result in a poor quality image, selecting too high a resolution can result in a too large a file, which will take too long to display or print.

Although we can adjust file size in Photoshop, some preliminary size assessment must also be made before we scan, to maintain a workable file.

As a rule of thumb, you can generally get a good master copy if you double the output resolution for the initial scan. In other words, for web projects, set the scan resolution to between 200-300 dpi, keeping in mind the size of the resulting file, the pixel dimensions, print size and file size, and how you may want to manipulate the image within Photoshop.

Printed in Great Britain
by Amazon.co.uk, Ltd.,
Marston Gate.